Rhine Guide

from Mainz to Koblenz

EHRENFELS UND DER MÄUSETHURM

Wolfgang Kootz / Willi Sauer / Willi Knopf

Edm. von König-Verlag, Heidelberg

Information

Aßmannshausen: Tel. (06722) 2615 or at the main office in Rüdesheim

Bacharach: Verkehrsamt, Oberstraße 1 (Postfach 47), Tel. (06743) 2968

Bad Salzig: Verkehrsamt, Tel. (06742) 6297

Bingen: Verkehrsamt, Rheinkai 21, 6530 Bingen/Rhein 1, Tel. 06721/142 69

Boppard: Städt. Verkehrsamt, Karmeliterstr. 2, 5407 Boppard, Tel. (06742) 1030

Braubach: Städt. Verkehrsamt, Rathausstr. 8, 5423 Braubach, Tel. (02627) 203

Brey: Rhein-Mosel-Eifel TOURISTIK, Bahnhofstraße 11 5400 Koblenz, Tel. (0261) 14024-6

Etltville: Verkehrsamt, Schmittstr. 10 (Postfach 89), 6228 Eltville, Tel. (06123) 5091

Ingelheim: Verkehrsamt im Rathaus, 6507 Ingelheim, Tel. (06132) 7041

Kamp-Bornhofen: Verkehrsamt im Rathaus, 5424 Kamp-Bornhofen, Tel. (06773) 360

Kaub: Verkehrsamt der Stadt, Schulstr. 33, Tel. (06774) 222

Koblenz: Fremdenverkehrsamt, 5400 Koblenz 1, Verkehrspavillon gegenüber dem Hauptbahnhof, Tel. (0261) 31304 and 33134

Lahnstein: Fremdenverkehrsamt, 5420 Lahnstein, Stadthallen-passage, Tel. (02621) 1033

Lorch: Städt. Verkehrsamt, Markt 5 (Postfach 1109), 6223 Lorch/Rhein, Tel. (06726) 318 and 317

Niederheimbach: Verkehrsverein, 6531 Niederheimbach, Tel. (06743) 6001

Main: Fremdenverkehrsverein, 6500 Mainz, Bahnhofsplatz, Tel. (06131) 233741

Oberwesel: Verkehrsamt, 6532 Oberwesel, Rathausstr. 3, Tel. (06744) 8131 and 304

Rhens: Rhein-Mosel-Eifel TOURISTIK, Bahnhofstraße 11, 5400 Koblenz, Tel. (0261) 14024-6

Rüdesheim: Verkehrsamt, Postfach 1269, Rheinstr. 16, 6220 Rüdesheim am Rhein, Tel. (06722) 2962

St. Goar: Verkehrsamt, 5401 St. Goar, Heerstr. 15, Tel. (06741) 383

St. Goarshausen: Städt. Verkehrsamt, Bahnhofstr. 126, 5422 St. Goarshausen, Tel. (06771) 427

Spay: Rhein-Mosel-Eifel TOURISTIK, Bahnhofstraße 11, 5400 Koblenz, Tel. (0261) 14024-6

Trechtingshausen: Verkehrsverein, Tel. (06721) 6411

Wiesbaden: Fremdenverkehrsamt, 6200 Wiesbaden, Wilhelmstr. 49 (Postfach 3840), Tel. (06121) 312847

The Rhine from Mainz to Koblenz

When it gets to Mainz, the Rhine changes direction from north to west, flowing on to Bingen where it is forced through a narrow valley cutting into the slate hills. It took the river millions of years to wear away the 200 - 300 m deep valley. The plateau-like hills are divided into four parts as a result of the deep cuts made by the rivers Rhine, Moselle and Lahn. The rocky Rhine valley was already an important traffic route – on the river and on land – in Roman times. It was from the Romans that the inhabitants learnt how to fortify their towns and, especially important, to cultivate vines on the sunny slopes. After having been elected in Frankfurt, 32 German Emperors and Kings passed through the Middle Rhine area on their way to the coronation in Aachen and showed themselves to the inhabitants there. Ships and rafts were navigated downstream with great difficulty and danger due to the many rapids and reefs, while on shore the travelling merchants were constantly in danger of being attacked by gangs of robbers. When the many castles were built, it became safer to travel by road, but not necessarily cheaper, as the castle owners expected payment in return for protection. Some levied tolls on their own authority, others had the right to charge customs duties as an Imperial fief, so there were ten customs places the merchant had to pay at between Bingen and Koblenz alone. No wonder there was conflict, no wonder many a castle owner was called a robber-baron. Such mischief flourished particularly in the 13th century when the Emperors had very little power, but after 1273 Kaiser Rudolf von Habsburg had the robbers' dens crushed and law and order restored.

Although the castles were originally built to control the owners' property, they also served to protect adjacent settlements. Some castles were also sovereign's residences, thus providing craftsmen, fishermen, farmers and winegrowers with a modest income. With the improvement of firearms in the 16th century, the castles became less significant. Only a few of them, such as Rheinstein and Ehrenbreitstein, were made into fortresses. Many others fell into decay, because the noblemen went to live in more comfortable palaces down in the valley, and were taken over as hiding places by thieves and gangs of robbers. The rest of the castles fell victim to the armies of Ludwig XIV and Napoleon. The only mediaeval castle left standing is the Marksburg.

Goethe's journey down the Rhine in 1774 was the start of the Age of Romanticism. From the beginning of the 19th century onwards, the Rhine valley became a centre of attraction for tourists from many European countries. This sudden interest in the historic ruins meant that attention was paid to preserving the structures and then to the castles being restored from 1825 onwards. Today most of them are open to the public and contain restaurants or museums. What makes this whole area so interesting and attractive for the visitor is not only the large number of castles, but also charming, old-world little towns surrounded by fortified walls, towers and gates, time-honoured churches with artistic burial monuments and neat wine-growing villages framed by sunny vineyards interspersed with steep walls of rock. Year after year millions of visitors are drawn to the romantic Middle Rhine area, which boasts more castles between Rüdesheim and Koblenz than any other region in the world.

Mainz

Even before Christian times there was an open settlement here alongside a walled legionary fortress. This was the headquarters of the Romans in Upper Germania. The «Roman Stones» in the Zahlbachtal (Zahlbach valley) and remains of pillars from their

Mainz: Modern buildings beside the Rhine with the two main spires of the thousand years old Cathedral towering above.

water system are reminders of that period, as are also those parts of the Roman city wall still standing. Boniface, Bishop of Mainz in the 8th century, bestowed on Mainz its important position with regard to this area's conversion to Christianity. Under his successor, Mainz advanced to becoming an archbishopric and was the only town apart from Rome to be granted the name «Holy See». Following this, the archbishops of Mainz were first given the title «Archchancellor of the Empire» (965) and then the chairmanship of the Electoral College (1257). In the 11th and 12th centuries, seven kings were crowned in the Cathedral, the church of the archbishops. For many decades, the citizens of the town put up great resistance to being ruled over by the archbishops, but in 1462 they were defeated by the Elector and Archbishop Adolf von Nassau. From then on Mainz remained the undisputed residence of Electoral Mainz with no self-government by the people. When the Elector fled to escape the French revolutionary troops in 1792, Electoral Mainz became a republic and in 1802 it was deprived of its archbishop's seat. In 1814 Mainz became part

Mainz Cathedral from the north-west. This church combines Ro-manesque, Gothic and Baroque architecture.

5

Mainz, Cathedral: Archbishops' epitaphs (16th cent.)

of Hessen and in 1950 it was chosen as the capital of the State of Rheinland-Pfalz (Rhineland-Palatinate). The Cathedral **(Dom)**, started under Archbishop Williges (975-1011), is the central point of the Old City. Its monumental size and importance is accentuated by the large squares in the surrounding area and the residences of the wealthy citizens around it. Like the old St. Peter's Cathedral in Rome, it has two transepts. In the fairly small chancel the lower storeys of the slim steeples with their spiral staircases date back to the original church. The Romanesque nave (12th century) connects the transepts, the higher western transept being of great artistic value. The lower floors of the 82.5 m high central tower were completed in 1239, the upper floor as far as the clock added in 1490 and the Baroque top in 1769-74. The architect of the final part was Michael Neumann, son of the famous Balthasar Neumann. The market portal (around 1200), today the entrance to the cathedral, has a two-sided bronze door (around 1000) with an inscription. Thick pillars of mighty blocks of limestone divide the 109 m long church into three aisles. The plain groined vaulting of the nave (29 m high) rises up to the domes of the central towers at a height of 38 and 44 metres.

The cathedral probably contains the best collection of 11th to 20th century epitaphs and statues. The most valuable in artistic terms are the memorial to Archbishop Johann II von Nassau (*1419), with which the so-called «Adalbertmeister» created the typical Gothic Mainz epitaph, as well as the works of the Mainz artist Hans Backoffen from the beginning of the 16th century. The imposing baptismal font of 1328 shows the 12 apostles, the Virgin Mary and St. Martin in relief pewter. On the market square in front of the cathedral

Renaissance fountain (1526) on the Cathedral Square

the **Renaissance fountain** of 1526 stands out with its magnificent variety of design and colouring. To the east of the cathedral we discover the unique printing museum with its exact reproduction of **Gutenberg's workshop.** Attractive Old City streets full of picturesque half-timbered houses and Baroque aristocratic mansions take us on to the defiant wooden-tower (14th century) to the east and then on to St. Stephan's Church with its impressive cloisters at the southern corner of the Old City. The **Electoral Castle** near the Rhine promenade can be considered one of the finest Renaissance buildings in all of Germany. It is today the home of the Roman-Germanic Central Museum.

The Victor Dativius Arch in the Castle Park provides an attractive view across to the Christuskirche.

Opposite the «Jubilee Fountain» at the south-west corner of the park stands St. Peter's Church. In the centre of the neighbouring «Deutschhausplatz» there is «Jupiter's Column», erected at the time of Roman settlement half way down to their port on the Rhine. The «Deutschhaus» on the northern side of the square is now the home of the state parliament of Rhineland Palatinate. The building standing on the corner where the Deutschhausgasse leads into the square is called the «Sautanz» and is today used by the Südwestfunk broadcasting institution. If we walk along this narrow street, the Deutschhausgasse, we reach the former arsenal, now government offices, with a Stresemann Memorial Hall. Not far away from here is the Natural History Museum.

From among the many events worth mentioning the most outstanding are the Mainz Carnival season with its festive meetings and the traditional Rosenmontagszug (carnival procession on the last Monday before Lent).

The «Wooden Tower» (14th century), one of the gates of the mediaeval town defences.

Wiesbaden

Wiesbaden, the capital of Hessen, owes its name as an international spa and congress centre to its favourable situation as regards transport facilities and to its **hot springs.** The so-called «Kochbrunnen» alone pours out 500,000 litres of warm salt water a day. As early as in the year 50 AD the existence of hot springs was mentioned by a Roman historian. In the following decades Roman baths were built within the settlement, and a wall around them was added about 370. But it was not until towards the end of the 17th century that the town rose to political importance, when the princes of Hessen-Nassau made it their second residence. Then in 1744 when the Nassau sovereign moved his place of residence to the castle of Wiesbaden-Biebrich, he emphasized the importance of his new metropolis.

The spa park borders on the Wilhelmstrasse and the Sonnenbergerstrasse. Near where the two roads meet, the **spa hotel and pump-room,** built in 1907, and the casino used to be the centre of spa activities. The springs and theatre colonnade together with the Hessen State Theatre complete the collection od 19th century Neo-Classical buildings in this area. The modern spa facilities have been moved out to Aukammtal. Opposite the State Theatre, the Burgstrasse leads us into the **Old City**. The slender main tower of the Neo-Gothic market church takes us on to the castle

Wiesbaden: Fountains in the park in front of the dome of the spa hotel (1907)

square, dominated by a building which was formerly the Nassau palace and now houses Hessen's State Parliament. The simple façade of the new town hall opposite is livened up by a portico. The old town hall, built in 1609, now serving as the registry office, is the oldest secular building in the town. Sandstone reliefs seem to extend the round-arched windows on the first floor right up to the cornice, thus matching the style of the three entrance doors

Wiesbaden: Market day on Castle Square. To the left of the market church is Hessen's State Parliament, the former Nassau Palace (1840); to the right, behind the lion fountain (1537), stands the new town hall with its portico.

above and beside the outside staircase. The market fountain (1537) in front of the building is decorated with a gold lion bearing his sovereign's coat of arms. Following the Marktstrasse and Langgasse we arrive at the Kranzplatz with the Hochbrunnen, the most famous and most productive of the 27 hot springs in Wiesbaden. The Geisberg on the northern side of the square and the Dambachtal lead us to the **Greek Chapel** – also called Russian Chapel – whose gold domes attract a large number of visitors. It was built on the slopes of the Neroberg between 1848 and 1855 by Herzog Adolph von Nassau as a memorial to his wife Elisabeth Michailowna, who died young. Since 1888, a hydraulic funicular railway has been taking visitors up to the top of Wiesbaden's Hausberg (245 m) with its fine view of the town, as well as to the Opelbad, an open-air swimming pool on the Neroberg.

Hessen's state metropolis offers its visitors the cultured atmosphere of a modern spa town. Apart from the modern spa facilities available, the town naturally also provides its spa guests and other visitors with a wide range of cultural and social events.

Eltville

On the northern bank of the Rhine from Wiesbaden to Rüdesheim we have the delightful Rheingau area, home of the world-famous Rhine wine and one of the most important wine-growing regions in Germany. Passing through the wine-growing village of Walluf we make our way to Eltville, the oldest town in the Rheingau. In the 14th and 15th centuries this was the residence of the archbishops and electors of Mainz. The **castle** was first destroyed in the «tariff war» (1301), was then rebuilt and finally fell a victim to **Swedish** troops in the Thirty Years' War. But the impressive hall-tower, today the home of the Gutenberg Mu-

For many centuries the Electoral Castle in Eltville was the residence of the Archbishops and Electors of Mainz. Its central point is the four-storey Hall Tower (14th century).

seum, with its tower platform and deep dungeon, are still standing. Also worth seeing are the numerous **domains** of court officials.

The Martinstor (St. Martin's Gate) and the Sebastiansturm (Sebastian's Tower) with the remains of the town wall battlements show how well-fortified the town was. The simple **town parish church** is considered to have the most important collection of Late Gothic art treasures in the Middle Rhine area including artistically valuable frescoes, epitaphs, Madonnas and chapels da-

«Burg Crass», a Romanesque nobleman's residence. Behind this the Hall Tower (14th century) of the Archbishops' castle.

ting back to 1400 onwards. The most valuable treasures are the Willigesstein (around 1000), a historical document, as well as the impressive baptismal stone crafted in 1517 in Hans Backoffen's workshop in Mainz. The quaint little streets in the old part of the town around the church are dominated by romantic half-timbered houses and large-scale Baroque buildings.

The towns of **Erbach, Hattenheim, Östrich** and **Winkel** are lined up on the right bank of the Rhine like pearls on a string. Just before we rech Hattenheim, a road turns off to **Eberbach Monastery** (4 km) founded by Cistercian monks in 1135. With its Romanesque church (12th century) the monastery is considered the most important mediaeval work of art in Hessen.

Hattenheim itself has one of the finest village squares in this part of the country. Besides the old town hall, attractive half-timbered houses and fine domains it also has an imposing ruined tower, the remains of the former castle of 1118.

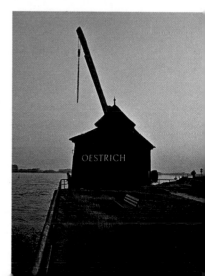

An old Rhine crane near Östrich

Ingelheim: The «Wehrkirche» with the ring-wall was part of the town fortifications in the Middle Ages.

Ingelheim

Halfway between Mainz and Bingen on a site of ancient civilization lies the little town of Ingelheim. Its greatest period in history started with Charlemagne's visit to Nieder-Ingelheim in 774. A Reichsversammlung (Imperial Assembly) was held here in 788, in the course of which Herzog Tassilo of Bavaria was sentenced to death, then pardoned and ordered to spend the rest of his days in a monastery. At about this time, Charlemagne started on the construction of the **Kaiser-Pfalz** (royal residence). The golden age of the Pfalz was under the Saxon kings, who chose it as their residence from 936 to 1043. In 1163 Kaiser Friedrich I «Barbarossa» resided in the Pfalz and had it made into a heavily fortified Reichsburg (Imperial fortress) and a memorial to Charlemagne. It finally lost its importance as a royal residence in 1354 when it became the seat of a collegiate church. A short time later the «Saal» area was made available for settlement. After this the «Reichsburg» had to undergo two stiff tests of its strength, but it both cases – in the sieges by Dieter von Isenburg (1460) and Landgraf Wilhelm II of Hessen (1504) – it proved able to stand up to the test and resist its attackers.

Remains of this probably most important secular building from the early Middle Ages can still be seen today in the evangelical parish church, the **Saalkirche,** first mentioned in 997 as a palace chapel. The figurative and ornamental decoration dates back to the time of the alterations made by Friedrich Barbarossa. The same applies to the unusual chancel. Also still standing are remains of the Carolingian Reichssaal (Imperial Hall) «Aula Regia» and of the outer ring wall with the ruins of the corner tower «Bolander» and a partly walled-up double archway, the Heidesheimer Tor.

The Roman Catholic parish church of **St. Remigius,** built from 1739 onwards in Baroque style, has an impressive Romanesque tower. Whereas the three plain lower storeys were built in the 12th century, the upper storeys and the tympans give evidence of the greater richness in style of the following century.

In the 14th/15th century **Ober-Ingelheim** was the main seat of the Oberhof, the imperial court of appeal. The town's defences with numerous towers and gate-towers are still in good condition, and some parts of the town still give a good impression of what it used to look like, e.g. «An der **Burgkirche**». What really is well worth seeing is the evangelical parish church, which has a ring wall round the fortified churchyard – in places double – and originally formed part of the town's defences, probably also serving as a place of refuge. The guard-house and the battlements of the Staufer church tower (12th century) indicate its significance as part of the town's fortifications. The chancel and the higher extension of the church were added after 1400. In the 15th - 17th centuries, the church was the burial ground of the noble families living in Ober-Ingelheim.

Two of the artistic monuments especially worth mentioning are those of Hans von Ingelheim (*1480) and Wilhelm von Ochenheim (*1465).

Ingelheim: Town wall with a fortified tower near the evangelical parish church (Wehrkirche)

The Niederwald Monument near Rüdesheim

From Rüdesheim and Assmannshausen there is a choice of foot-paths, roads and **cable railways** leading to the top of the Nieder-wald. On the edge of the forest, 225 m above the Rhine, a huge monument designed to symbolize the re-establishment of the German Empire and Germany's unity was erected between 1877

The Niederwald Monument near Rüdesheim: 37.6 m high, erec-ted 1877-83 to commemorate «the re-establishment of the Ger-man Empire».

The Niederwald Monument: bronze relief with the life-size figures of Kaiser Wilhelm I on horseback, Bismarck, the German princes and sovereigns and their commanders-in-chief as well as soldiers from all branches of the armed forces.

and 1883. The main figure on the 37.6 m high monument is the «Germania», 10.5 m tall, bearing the Imperial sword and the German Emperor's crown. 32 tons of bronze were required for casting the weight lady, which greatly accounts for the total cost of 1.2 m gold marks. More than 1 million was donated by the people. The sandstone base has a bronze relief showing nearly 200 life-size figures: Kaiser Wilhelm I on horseback, Bismarck, the German princes and sovereigns and their commanders-in-chief as well as soldiers from all branches of the armed forces. Two angels «War» and «Peace», each 2.8 m high, stand on either side of the statue.

Near the monument there is a breeding and training centre for eagles, which contains a large variety of native birds of prey. From the monument we have a wonderful view across the vineyards right down to Rüdesheim, and across the Rhine to Bingen and Burg Klopp, situated at the mouth of the River Nahe. Looking upstream along the Rhine we see the beautiful Rheingau area; many have sung the praises of this region with its gentle slopes where wine was already being cultivated by Roman veterans 2000 years ago. Looking downstream we see that both the river and the valley become narrower, which marks the beginning of the steep and rugged Middle Rhine section. Well-kept and well-marked footpaths lead into the Niederwald national park, to the hunting lodge or to the St. Hildegard Benedictine Convent (1900-04) with its interesting Beuron-style church and a magnificent view of the Rhine valley from the Convent gardens.

Rüdesheim

Cable-railway Rüdesheim-Niederwald-Monument. On the right the keep of the Brömserburg.

Just a few kilometres past the town the Rhine abruptly changes direction and becomes narrower. This point, the so-called **Binger Loch,** used to be unnavigable because of its many sandbanks and rapids. So ships going north were unloaded in Rüdesheim, the goods taken to Lorch along the old Celtic road and then put on board ship again there. These reloading activities brought the town trade and thus a welcome source of income. It was not until the 11th century, when the shipping channel was widened for the first time, that ships were able to navigate past this extremely dangerous point. But even nowadays it still has its hazards and many navigators from other parts prefer to hire a pilot for the stretch between Rüdesheim and St. Goar. Right next to the Rhine and extending into the water we find the **Brömserburg,** the oldest and best preserved of Rüdesheim's three castles. From the 10th to the 13th century it served the archbishops of Mainz at times as living quarters and as a refuge.

After the archbishops gave it as a fief to the knights «von Rüdesheim» in the 13th century, for a short time it developed into a fearful robber's den. In the Sponheim feud (1281) Archbishop Wernherr von Mainz totally defeated the knights of Rüdesheim and their Sponheim allies. The castle's present name came from the collateral line «Brömser von Rüdesheim», who lived in the castle from 1548 until the line died out in 1668. After 1810 the aristocratic family «von Ingelheim» had it renovated and since then visitors' books have been kept. The oldest such book shows that Goethe stayed there in 1814. Today the castle belongs to the town and houses the Rheingau folk and wine museum with a large collection of drinking vessels.

The **Boosenburg,** formerly called Oberburg, belonged to the Rüdesheim «Füchse» family. The only part still preserved is the defiant castle tower. The market square tower was once part of the Vorderburg, the centrepoint of the inner town defences. In the Oberstrasse we can still see some of the old **aristocratic residences** such as the Ritter'schen Hof (No. 4), the Bassenheimer Hof (No. 5) and the Brömser Hof (No. 27). Heinrich Brömser had the Brömser Hof built in 1542 and decorated with fresco paintings. In the chapel these show a large combined coat-of-arms of the two families Brömser and Greiffenclau, in the ancestral hall there is the «Ahnenprobe» giving evidence of the family's knightly extraction. The coat-of-arms on the courtyard gate was put up around 1650 by Heinrich Brömser, the last male descendant of this aristocratic Rüdesheim family (*1668), court judge and Privy Councillor of Electoral Mainz. Today the Brömser Hof houses «Siegfried's mechanical musical cabinet», a collection of self-playing musical instruments covering three centuries. The Roman Catholic parish church (14th century) on the market square strangely flies a weather-vane with a half-moon and a star. This is said to have been installed by a Ritter (knight) von Brömser, who took part in one of the crusades. In many of Rüdesheim's romantic narrow streets with their cosy wine taverns, many of which sell their own wines, the many visitors can be seen strolling around and stopping to drink a glass of wine or more. One of the most famous streets is the **Drosselgasse.** With

Rüdesheim: Rheinstrasse and Niederwald-Monument.

a population of only 8000, Rüdesheim can accommodate more than 5000 tourists. The town's second most important source of income is wine-growing, in particular the famous Riesling-grape wine, sparkling wines and brandy. The **Adlerturm** (Eagle's Tower) (15th century) at the western end of the Rheinstrasse was once part of the towns' mediaeval defences. The 20.4 m high tower used to be situated right beside the Rhine. It was from here

Rüdesheim: The Brömserburg (around 1000), used in the 13th century by robber-barons as a hiding-place after highway robbery and plundering.

that notice of the first drifting ice was passed on downstream by means of semaphore and fire signals. The ground floor, which has walls one meter thick, used to be a dungeon, only accessible through a first-floor trap-door. A bronze plaque on one of the outer walls commemorates Goethe's visit to Rüdesheim in 1814. The peak season for international tourism in Rüdesheim is from the end of May to the end of October. The highlights of this are the magnificent firework display «The Magic of the Rhine on Fire round the Binger Loch» and the traditional Rüdesheim Wine Festival (mid-August). Wine and Sekt cellars as well as a famous brandy distillery are open to the public on weekdays at any time.

18

Rüdesheim: The most famous street in the Middle Rhine area, the Drosselgasse. Cosy wine taverns, with and without music, give the visitor a lasting impression of Rhenish hospitality and gaiety. The Drosselgasse is so narrow that, after one glass of wine too many, visitors may find that the walls on the right and left come in handy on their way home.

19

▲ Mäuseturm and ruins of Ehrenfels

▼ Drosselgasse

▲ Niederwald Monument

▼ Rüdesheimer Winzerexpress

▲ Drosselhof ▼ Drosselgasse by night

Bingen and Burg Klopp

South of the Nahe mouth on the outer bend of the Rhine lies the ancient city of Bingen. Here, 2000 years ago, the Romans built a citadel they called «Bingium» at an intersection of two trade routes, and the first settlement probably grew up here for reasons of protection. A Christian community is mentioned as early as in the 5th century. In 983, the Emperor Otto II made over this area by the mouth of the Nahe to his Chancellor, Archbishop Williges of Mainz. In the tariff war of 1301, King Albrecht I's troops besieged and conquered Bingen and destroyed its castle. With this war the King broke the power of the Rheinish electors for a few years and forced them to remove the lucrative customs duties levied along the Rhine. But when Albrecht was assassinated in 1308 the levying of duties started up again immediately.

The town's landmark is **Burg Klopp,** situated on a hill in the middle of the town. Probably built in Roman times, it was the seat of noblemen during the period when the archbishops were in power. In the tariff war (1301) the castle troops only surrendered when fire made further defence seem pointless. This gave the castle its title of honour «Burg Klopp the Invincible». After destruction by the French soldiers of Louis XIV in 1689 the castle

Bingen with Bingerbrück on the other side of the River Nahe. In the background, the «Mäuseturm» at «Binger Loch».

Burg Klopp above Bingen. Probably of Roman origin. Today seat of the town council and a folk museum.

had only just been more or less repaired when its owner, the Cathedral Chapter of Mainz had the castle blown up «to prevent its being used as a base in later wars». After 1875 it was rebuilt in the style of 15th century Rhine castles. In 1897 the town bought the castle and since this time it has served as the town hall and a folk museum. Above the gatehouse entrance there is a coat-of-arms of the Cathedral Chapter of Mainz. One of the most interesting things worth seeing in the museum is a collection of Roman doctor's instruments (2nd century).

The foundations of the keep and the 52 m deep castle-well probably date back to Roman times.

Open to visitors: 1.4. to 15.10. daily

View across the Nahe to Bingen and Burg Klopp.

The ruins of Burg Ehrenfels, which once stretched right down to a customs house beside the Rhine. At the mouth of the Nahe, Bingen (left) and Bingerbrück.

The Mäuseturm and the ruins of Burg Ehrenfels

On the Rhine island at Binger Loch the pretty little **Mäuseturm** strikes our eye. It was probably built in the 13th century as a look-out tower for Ehrenfels Castle, which in spite of its towers and outworks had no view of the Rhine to the north. This is where the tower's name came from since «mausen» means to be on the lookout, the way a cat is on the lookout for a mouse. Legend,

however, has another interpretation: the hardhearted Bishop Hatto is said to have sought refuge in the tower from a horde of mice; in vain, the mice swam after him and devoured him.

The tower and Ehrenfels castle were partly destroyed by Swedish troops in 1636 and then completely ruined by the French in 1689. The «Romanticist on the Throne», King Friedrich Wilhelm of Prussia, had the base of the outwork propped up and re-

The «Mäuseturm» (13th century), once a lookout-tower for Burg Ehrenfels.

paired and then the tower rebuilt in 1855 in Neo-Gothic style. From then on until 1974 the tower served Rhine navigation purposes as a signal station.

The ruin in the midst of the vineyards above the Mäuseturm is what is left of Burg **Ehrenfels.** The castle, along with its subsidiary buildings, used to stretch right down to the Rhine, the final building right next to the river being the customs house. It was built around 1215 as a customs fortress and passed into the possession of the archbishops of Mainz around 1270. Because of its strategic importance, the archbishops hat it reinforced many times and used it as a hiding place for Cathedral treasures in times of war. Ehrenfels has remained a ruin since it was destroyed by the French (1689). With its mighty curtain wall facing the hillside flanked by towers, it is one of the most impressive constructions along the Rhine.

30 min. walk from Rüdesheim, 15 min. from the level crossing. Beautiful view. Inside not open to the public due to danger of collapse.

Assmannshausen

The romantic village of Assmannshausen, famous for its red wines and situated only a few kilometres downstream from Ehrenfels castle, today is part of the town of Rüdesheim. Built as

The view from the lookout-point «Schweizerhaus» down on to Assmannshausen. The fortified tower of the Late Gothic parish church was the corner-stone of the town's defences.

Assmannshausen: romantic half-timbered house in the town centre.

a Franconian settlement, it was first mentioned officially in 1108 as «Hasemannshusen». A partially preserved ring-wall overlooking the Rhine once served to protect the town from hostile invasion and drifting ice. The cornerstone of the town fortifications was the Late Gothic church guard-tower. The church contains an altar-piece and a madonna, both 15th century works of art.

Along the narrow streets of the town centre picturesque half-timber houses are huddled together, not far from the sun-baked slopes of the «Höllenberg». Here, on the bluish-red phyllite slate of the Taunus area, one of the best German «Spätburgunder» wines is cultivated.

A chair-lift to the Niederwald monument, a hunting lodge and numerous footpaths and splendid vantage points also make the tiny wine-growing village an ideal place to visit, either for a holiday or just for a day out.

Assmannshausen: historical restaurant beside the Rhine.

Burg Rheinstein

Across the Rhine from Assmannshausen Burg Rheinstein with its battlements rises up from a rocky, craggy ridge. Built around 900 as a customs house for the Empire, it was given in about 990 by Emperor Otto III to the archbishopric of Mainz, which had it extended into a fortress. The most significent event in its history was when Kaiser Rudolf von Habsburg sat in judgement upon the «insubordinate» knights of Reichenstein, Sooneck and Ehrenfels. By the 17th century,

*Burg Rheinstein: former Imperial custom fortress. First castle
to be rebuilt in the 19th century.*

the castle had fallen into disrepair and was described as a ruin.
Prince Friedrich Wilhelm of Prussia bought it in 1825 and it was
one of the first castles he had rebuilt in the following years.
*Open (guided tours) daily. Footpath from carpark below the
castle 5 minutes, from Trechtingshausen 2 km.*

Burg Reichenstein

About 2 km past Burg Rheinstein at the entrance to the town of Trechtingshausen we discover the Clemens Chapel beside the Rhine. Built in the 13th century, this is one of the oldest churches along the Rhine, and on the other side of the Rhine, perched on a rocky ridge, we see Burg Reichenstein, one of the oldest castles (11th century). In 1253 this robber knight's castle was destroyed by the Rheinischer Städtebund (Rhenish Town Alliance). In 1282 Rudolf von Habsburg had this robber's den destroyed again and the robbers executed near the Clemens Chapel. In 1899 it was bought by Baron von Kirsch-Puricelli and renovated.

Like Ehrenfels Castle, Burg Reichenstein also has a mighty curtain wall flanked by two towers instead of a central keep. This wall is 8 m thick at its base, 5 m thick at the top and 16 m high. Inside there is now a hotel-restaurant. The other rooms contain valuable furniture and a remarkable collection of arms and antlers.

Open to the public (guided tours) January - October. Carpark in castle yard. Footpath from the Rhine 5 min.

Castles Sooneck, Heimburg and Fürstenberg

The village of Trechtingshausen, which is well worth seeing, still possesses remains of a medieval sentry wall on the Rhine, a romantic gate in Neuweg and a crenelated round tower. Just as Reichenstein, situated above the village, so the neighbouring castle of Sooneck also belonged to robber bands and which

Burg Reichenstein (11th century) above Trechtingshausen.

Castle Sooneck near Trechtingshausen. Built in the early 11th century. Twice destroyed as a nest of robber barons in 1253 and 1282.

were destroyed on two occasions during the 13th century. The emperor lifted a temporary ban on building in the year 1349, and the new owner, Kurmainz, had the castle re-erected. In 1689, it fell victim to storming French troops and in the 19th century, Crown Prince Friedrich Wilhelm of Prussia commissioned it to be rebuilt in the romantic style.

The sleepy village of Niederheimbach lies sprawled out on its narrow stretch of bank on the Rhine, and just a little above its roofs one perceives Kurmainz Heimburg in all its splendour, built in or about 1300 as a northern bastion against the territories of the dukes of the Palatine. Later, the castle fell into decay, but was rebuilt in the 19th century. One notices with interest the strong, ivy-bedecked curtain walling and the 25 metre high keep. Castle Fürstenberg above Rheindiebach was erected by the Archbishop of Cologne both to protect his property and also his right to exact duties and taxes in the year 1200. It has remained in ruins since its destruction in 1689. The tapered keep, crowned by crenelated battlements is still in good condition.

Conducted tours of Burg Sooneck only from March to September. The way there on foot is about one kilometre.

Lorch

On the opposite side, where the River Wisper joins the Rhine, we find the wine-growing town of Lorch below the Nollich ruins (pre-1100). The Gothic parish church (started in the 13th century) contains ancient epitaphs and an artistically styled high altar.

Bacharach

Together with Burg Stahleck, Bacharach became part of Count Palatinate property in the 11th century. Its important wood and wine trade as well as its customs duties made Bacharach alongside Kaub one of the wealthiest towns in the whole of the Palatinate. The **town fortifications** (14th century) are the best preser-

Bacharach: The well-preserved towers of the town's mediaeval fortifications, St. Peter's parish church (from 1100 onwards), the ruins of the Werner Chapel (1294) and Burg Stahleck are the sights most worth seeing.

ved in the Middle Rhine area together with those of Oberwesel. It is possible to walk along the whole length of the sentry walk on the Rhine front, seven of the towers are still fully preserved, even the connenting wall to the castle as a kind of corner-stone is still standing. The former customs bastion jutting out into the Rhine at the southern end of the town was converted into a Capuchin monastery around 1700, and the church of this monastery is still standing. The main St. Peter's Church was built in around 1100 and contains valuable mediaeval frescoes.

There are many **half-timbered façades** to be admired, of which perhaps the old Post Office, with its splendid courtyard, and the «Old House» (1568) on the market square are most worthy of mention. Halfway up to the castle we find the striking ruins of the Gothic **Werner Chapel,** which was built from 1294 onwards over a period of 140 years. The district of **Steeg,** 1 km away from the Rhine, has not only a large number of picturesque half-timbered houses but also an interesting 14th century church with mediaeval frescoes. In former times Burg Stahlberg (13th century), watched over Steeg and the valley; today the castle is in ruins.

Burg Stahleck

There has been documentary evidence of Lords of Stahleck Castle since the beginning of the 12th century. In 1142 Hermann von Stahleck became Count Palatinate. In the following decades he and his successors completed the «Palatinate Barrier», consisting of the castles of Gutenfels, Pfalzgrafenstein, Stahleck, Stahlberg and Fürstenberg.

Bacharach: the «Old House» (1568), one of the many picturesque half-timbered houses in the old part of the town.

Burg Stahleck above Bacharach, seat of the Count Palatine in the 12th century and important corner bastion against the other Rhenish Electors.

This meant that this strategically important area where four territories of the Rhenish Electors met was more or less secure. Burg Stahleck was rebuilt after the Thirty Year's War, only to be wrecked again by French troops in 1689. The «Rheinischer Verein» (Rhineland Association) had it restored on its old foundations in 1925-27 as a youth hostel. The basic construction of the round keep in the middle of the castle yard dates back to the 12th century. The 14th century ring-wall becomes stronger on the side of attack to form a curtain wall flanked by corner towers. The entrance to the castle yard leads across a bridge – formerly a drawbridge – through the outer castle gate, the outer bailey and the inner gate. The keep (Palas) on the eastern side with its mighty hip-roof was reconstructed in 1931. The half-timbered buildings are still used as a youth hostel.

Car park. Footpath from Bacharach 25 min. Open by arrangement.

Bacharach: the ruins of the Gothic Werner Chapel (from 1294 onwards). On the right St. Peter's parish church (from 1100).

Kaub with the «Pfalz» and Burg Gutenfels

The town was first mentioned in 983 when it fell to the Archbishopric of Mainz. At the beginning of the 13th century the town, the right to collect customs duties on the Rhine and the castle – then mentioned for the first time – were in the hands of the Herren (Lords) von Falkenstein, who, however, sold their property to the Palatinate in 1277, which Kaub remained part of until 1802. In 1326 King Ludwig der Bayer («the Bavarian») resided in the castle. Around this time the island fortress **«Pfalzgrafenstein»** – in short «Pfalz» – must already have been under construction, as a year later Pope John XXII called on the archbishops of Mainz, Cologne and Trier to destroy the tower erected on an island on the Rhine near Kaub. A stone memorial tablet on the former Palatinate town hall commemorates the successful defence of Kaub in 1504, when the castle and town were besieged for 6½ weeks by the Landgrave Wilhelm von Hessen. The valiant way the castle was defended gave it the name **«Gutenfels»**. It also gave rise to the legend and the historical play about «Elslein von Kaub». Kaub's fateful hour came on New Year's Eve 1813/14 when the Prussian Field Marshal **Blücher** crossed the Rhine here in pursuit of Napoleon.

Burg Gutenfels above Kaub. On the Rhine island «Falkenaue», the former customs bastion Pfalzgrafenstein, called «Pfalz».

The «Pfalz» near Kaub, with Burg Gutenfels in the background.

*Kaub: The Blücher Memorial on the Rhine Promenade symboli-
zes Napoleon's being «thrown out» of Germany 1813/14. Above
the legendary «marshal Onwards» stands Burg Gutenfels
(around 1200).*

The Blücher Museum in his former quarters at 6, Metzgergasse
is open to the public every day except Monday and contains a
collection of arms and uniforms from that period. The Blücher
memorial owes its location on the Rhine promenade to a natural
disaster: a landslide in 1876 cost 26 lives and wrecked 10 houses

but it left behind a wider bank along the Rhine. Beside the memorial stands the Kaub water-level registration tower. Part of the mediaeval fortifications are still standing, e.g. the «Round Tower» in the east of the Old Town. At the western boundary of Old Kaub we find the Romanesque Wesel gate-tower. In the town itself the romantic streets «Auf der Mauer» and «Metzgergasse» as well as the Palatinate town hall with its coat-of-arms of the Electoral family are worthy of mention. The evangelical and Roman Catholic church under one roof grew up out of a late Romanesque church building. Until 1770 the Catholics celebrated their Mass in the chancel but then this was replaced by a new building in Late Rococo style. On a rocky crag behind the church is perched the bell-tower.

Customs duties being levied in Kaub were first mentioned in 1257. At that time there was a customs house on the flat Rhine island «Falkenaue». The five-sided, six-storey tower of the **«Pfalzgrafenstein»**, a castle built as a customs house in the middle of the Rhine, was started in about 1325; from 1340 onwards a 12 m high ring-wall in the shape of a ship's hull was put up around it. The outer wall shows a stone lion bearing the coat-of-arms of the Palatinate. Behind this there are gun bastions and several-storeyed wooden arcades with a sentry-walk. A portcullis in the ring-wall additionally fortified the entrance. Even today the entrance to the tower is on the third floor. What is especially interesting is the old castle dungeon, the floor of which could be raised and lowered depending on the water level.

Open to the public March - October, except Monday.

Above the «Pfalz» rises up the older of the two castles, **Burg Gutenfels,** built around 1200 by the Falkenstein family. It was in the King's Hall in 1287 that Burgrave Adolf von Nassau received news of the fact that he had been chosen to succeed Rudolf von Habsburg as king. A mural painting in this room depicts the announcement of this by heralds. The main construction with a 35 m high keep, the Palas (living quarters), the armoury and the inner castle yard is well preserved. The ring-wall dates back to the 14th century. In 1806 Napoleon had the castle defences removed and the castle put up for auction to be demolished. An archivist prevented its complete demolition by buying the ruins. After 1888 the architect Walter had it rebuilt. Today it is considered one of the most attractive and spacious castles along the Rhine and is the home of a hotel.

3 km footpath and road from Kaub. Not open to the general public.

Schönburg Castle and Oberwesel

Within view of Kaub the little town of Oberwesel snuggles into a little opening of the Rhine Valley. Surrounded by gently sloping vineyards, the town and its tower defences is proud of its appropriate nickname «town of many towers and wine». High above its silhouette, the majestic, thousand year old **Schönburg** keeps watch over the town. At one time the possession of the Grafen (Counts) von Stahleck, it was given in 1166 by Friedrich I «Barbarossa» to one of his officials as an imperial fief. He and his descendants then called themselves «von Schönburg» after the name of their residence. The customs duties on the Rhine in Oberwesel made them one of the richest and most powerful families in this region. 100 years after the granting of the fief, five families with the name «von Schönburg» already lived in the fortress, and in the 14th century it was extended into a spacious family castle called Ganerbenburg. It remained in this family until it was destroyed by the troops of King Louis XIV «Le Roi Soleil». After 1885 its owners had it partly rebuilt. Since then one part of the spacious castle has been used as and International Youth Hostel, another part as a hotel.

Footpath from Oberwesel 30 minutes. Car park beside the castle. Open to the public daily.

An impressive part of the structure is the mighty curtain wall on the side of the castle looking uphill. Behind this wall the division into three parts, with two keeps and one tower with living quarters, is clearly recognizable.

Schönburg Castle near Oberwesel. Its owners, the Lords of Schönburg, had it extended into a spacious family residence after 1166.

The **town** itself is situated on the site of an old Celtic settlement (400 BC) and a Roman military service point. In 1237 Schönburg Castle became subject to the Emperor alone, and Oberwesel, formerly Wesel, was able to pay 300 marks in silver and thus rid itself of Schönburg rule. In this way it became a free imperial town. In the following years the circumvallation was replaced by a city wall; with its 18 towers it is the most complete city wall still standing in the whole Middle Rhine area. Its massive solid round towers beside the Rhine, the Ochsenturm (Oxen Tower) and the

Oberwesel has the most complete and best-preserved mediaeval town fortifications in the Middle Rhine area. It has 18 fortified towers still standing. Rising up above the roofs of the town the Gothic churches of St. Martin (right) and «Liebfrauen» (Church of Our Lady).

Haagsturm are particularly worth seeing. The dainty little Werner **Chapel** and the now-ruined Franciscan monastery were also built in the same century. After 1300, with the help of the wealthy **Herren** (Lords) von Schönburg, the two Gothic collegiate churches «Liebfrauen» (Our Lady) and «St. Martin» were built, both of which contain valuable works of art, signs of the wealth of the **town**. The famous organ in the slender Liebfrauenkirche is especially worth mentioning.

The Loreley

Still today, mention of the Romance of the Rhine conjures up a picture of the mighty slate rock between Kaub and St. Goarshausen called the Loreley. Downstream the river was squeezed into its narrowest and deepest point; even in the 19th century, reefs and rapids made it extremely dangerous for ships and rafts to pass this point, so a «three bells» warning told the crew it was time to pray. Moreover the rock was already famous in the early

View of the narrow valley of the Middle Rhine area. The most striking point is the steep, outjutting «Loreley» rock in the centre of the picture.

Middle Ages for its good echo, thought to be ghostly voices. No wonder a multitude of legends was woven around the rock, the most famous of which is that of siren called «Loreley», who bewitches the hearts of sailors with her unearthly beauty and her enchanting voice. The sailors look up at the rock to catch sight of

The «Loreley»: The legendary slate rock rises up almost vertically to 132 m above water-level.

the charming maiden, forgetting for just a moment the dangerous rapids and reefs. Their boat is dashed to pieces and they sink beneath the waves for ever. This is what happened also to the young Erbgraf (heir to the Count's title) von Rheinpfalz, who is lured to his doom in this way. His father orders that the witch on the rock be caught or killed. When soldiers bar the way back into her cave, she calls on her father, the Rhine, to help her. Huge, foaming waves rise up out of the waters and carry the maiden away. Since then she has never been seen again. But sometimes, when the moon is shining bright, a mysterious singing is to be heard, described by Romanticist poets. Heinrich Heine's Song of Loreley, set to music by Silcher, made the Loreley Rock famous all over the world.

There is a footpath up to the top of the rock from the car park at the foot of the Loreley; alternatively the road can be taken from St. Goarshausen right up to the peak. A magnificent and unforgettable view is to be had from here of some of Germany's most famous scenery. The well-kept outdoor theatre from the Third Reich is used for many different events. Near the Berghotel we see the remains of a rampart originally part of a Celtic place of refuge.

Burg «Katz»

The siren «Loreley», who lured sailors to their doom with her unearthly beauty and her bewitching singing.

After the Counts of Katzenelnbogen had built Burg Rheinfels above St. Goar in the middle of the 13th century, they then had «Neukatzenelnbogen» Castle, «Katz» for short, erected on the other side of the Rhine in 1371. It served to reinforce Rheinfels Castle, safeguarded the crossing-point to its training-grounds, defended the little town of Hausen, and made it possible to give early warning of ships coming round the Loreley. With its «sister» it thus provided an effective barrier across the river above all aimed at defending its right to levy customs duties. The steep walls of the rocky ledge the castle stands on provided protection on three sides. On the side towards the hill, the Counts had a deep moat hewn into the rock. The stone bridge, which led into the long bailey, could be blown up in times of war. The side open to attack was also protected by means of a 40 m high keep. Strong fortified walls connected the keep on both sides with the living quarters, the five-sided Palas, across the protective steep hillside. The thick outer walls of the Palas as well as a slightly lower triangular bastion in front of it additionally fortified the castle, which was very likely impregnable before the arrival of firearms. The three-storey Palas contained not only the Burggrafenstufe and a number of lady's rooms and chambers but also two magnificent halls. From the benches within the projecting round towers the inhabitants had to splendid view of the river and the town. In the storage-cellars was the wine that added spice to the banquets. From the halls there were doors to the sentry walks and from there to the keep, which was a final place of refuge in case of emergency. Only the ground floor, the castle dungeon, could be reached from the courtyard. A spiral staircase let into the wall overlooking the courtyard connected the five upper storeys. The octagonal top floor with its look-out bays was the tower guards' abode. The other floors were inhabited and even had a fire-place. The keep and the staircase up the side of the Palas as well as the building for the kitchen and the bakery took up quite a lot of space within the fortified walls, in addition to which there was the well for drinking water in the centre of the courtyard.

The defending troops consisted of the commander (called Burggraf – burgrave – in the Middle Ages) and 50 to 80 mercenaries. In times of crisis reinforcement was called for and the citizens of the town were required to accommodate and feed the troops free of charge. Napoleon had the castle blown up in 1806, but it was rebuilt at the turn of the century. Later extensions by various owners changed the original mediaeval appearance of the castle. Today it is a convalescent home.

Footpath from St. Goarshausen 20 min. Open on request.

Burg «Katz» above St. Goarshausen, started in 1393 in order to reinforce the main castle «Rheinfels» opposite.

43

St. Goarshausen

The fishing village of St. Goarshausen became the property of the powerful Grafen von Katzenelnbogen in 1284. Soon after it became a town (1324), the 200 or so inhabitants started to erect a fortified town wall. On the side next to the Rhine they built a 230 m long, 11 m high construction, which also protected them

St. Goarshausen with Burg Katz: the magnificent firework display and Bengal illuminations called «The Rhine on Fire» (Rhein in Flammen).

from flooding and drifting ice. The east tower and the market tower are still standing. They flanked the Rhine promenade and shielded the two town-gates at the same time. From here the walls went uphill and with the «Katz» formed a defence triangle. The town itself consisted of two rows of houses on either side of the only road there was room for between the river and the rocky hillside. Still today there are attractive half-timbered houses in the «Grosse Burggasse». Houses no. 41-43 were originally the town hall (1532), which also housed the school and a teacher's flat. The square in front, called the Plan, was the market place and as such the centre of social life in the town. At no. 44 a slate

44

flight of steps branches off, leading to the old church and the churchyard. On the round market tower there is an unusual weather vane. The tower stands on the alluvial land of the Forstbach (forest brook) and over the years it has developed into the «leaning tower of St. Goarshausen». It is now inclined at an angle of 41 cm to the east and as much as 63 cm to the north. The square east tower was built directly on the rocky banks and was originally 23 m high. When the road was built, however, the surface level was raised, so that now the former ground floor with the dungeon is below ground and the entrance to the first floor is now on ground level. The four inhabitable storeys of the tower were burnt out in 1873.

4 km from St. Goarshausen on the slopes of the Hasenbachtal (Hasenbach Valley) we find the **Reichenberg** ruins (14th century), of great importance in castle history. It is the Katzenelnbogen family's third castle in this area. A wide curtain wall is flanked by two round towers. The remains of the 3-storey Palas (Hall building) have an almost classical appearance due to the fact that the ceilings have collapsed and three times three pillars left standing on top of each other bearing a high ribbed vault.

No viewing inside due to danger of collapse

St. Goarshausen: Walk along the Rhine Promenade, in the background Burg «Neukatzenelnbogen», called «Katz» for short.

45

View of Burg Katz, with St. Goar and Burg Rheinfels in the background.

St. Goar

The sister towns of St. Goarshausen and St. Goar are connected by a car ferry. Both owe their name to St. Goar, who lived as a hermit in the 6th century where the collegiate church of St. Goar now stands on the site of the chapel he built. By 765 the Saint's hermitage had grown into one of Germany's oldest monasteries. In the 12th century the Katzenelnbogen family acquired control of the monastery and the settlement as well as the right to levy duties on the Rhine in St. Goar. Being a fortified town, it was often involved in military conflicts such as the unsuccessful sieges of 1255/56, 1320, 1322, as well as several times in the Thirty Years' War and particularly in the Seven Years' War when altogether 81 houses, the hospital and the town hall were wrecked as a result of an explosion (1759) and arson by Irish soldiers (1761).

From the battlements of the **Stiftskirche** (Collegiate Church) the militia marksman Kretsch came up with a legendary bull's-eye when he wounded the French General Tallard so badly that his troops stopped the siege.

Beneath the chancel of the Stiftskirche is the Goarskapelle, a po-

pular place for pilgrims until the Reformation. The inside of the church is decorated with Gothic mural paintings and delicate net vaulting, a beautiful pillar pulpit and three magnificent monuments to the Landgraf (landgrave) Philipp II von Hessen-Rheinfels

St. Goar: View of the Stiftskirche (started in 1444). Of the original 8th century church the tomb of St. Goar is still preserved.

and his wife and also to Countess Adelheid von Katzenelnbogen (*1329). The smaller Roman Catholic parish church contains a 14th century Goar epitaph, which once served as a tombstone in the Goarkapelle. A Gothic triptych (around 1470) from the school of the «Hausbuchmeister» forms the centrepiece of the valuable high altar. The bell-tower is the former Koblenzer Tor (Koblenz Gate) containing a second Goar piece. The only parts of the town wall still standing are on the side towards the hill, towered over by the Hexenturm (Witches' Tower) and the Kanzleiturm (Chancellor's Tower).

Once a year on the third Saturday in September the two towns arrange a magnificent firework display called **«Rhein in Flammen»** (The Rhine on Fire). The towns and their castles are illuminated by Bengal lights and fireworks are set off from the castle towers.

Mediaeval depiction of St. Goar

St. Goar with its harbour and the castle ruins of Rheinfels. Opposite the sistertown of St. Goarshausen with Burg Katz.

49

Burg Rheinfels

Construction of the main structure of the castle was started in 1245 by Graf Dieter V von Katzenelnbogen. Only ten years later it was able to stand its first test when it was attacked by 9000 soldiers of the Rheinischer Städtebund (Rhenish Town Alliance) because of an increase in customs duties on the Rhine. After 40

Model of Rheinfels fortress according to plans of the surveyor Dilich, made in 1607. On the left the basic castle and the residential buildings, on the right towards the hillside the extensive fortifications.

unsuccessful charges and a siege lasting more than a year they were forced to withdraw empty-handed. When the powerful Katzenelnbogen family died out, the landgraves of Hessen acquired Rheinfels Castle in 1479, and from the 15th century onwards they added outworks and underground passages to fortify it as well as new living quarters. In the Palatinate War of Succession, Rheinfels Castle with 4000 men was the only fortress along the Rhine to withstand in 1692/93 the assault of a French army of 28,000 troops with 56 pieces of artillery. In 1758 the meanwhile neglected castle fell into enemy hands for the first time when the soldiers capitulated to French troops without a fight. Again in 1794, despite the fact that he was well equipped and had 3200 men under arms, a weak commander surrendered the fortress without a struggle which then fell into the hands of poorly-armed French revolutionary forces. He was later sentenced to death for this. In 1797/98 the French blew up the fortifications and the castle. The ruins were used as a quarry to provide stones for the rebuilding of Ehrenbreitstein fortress near Koblenz for example, until the Prince of Prussia bought it in 1843 and saved it from falling into complete decay.

A walk around the extensive ruins with their maze of several-storey sentry walks and underground passages gives us an excellent impression of the one time most powerful fortress along the Rhine. The underground passages beneath the outworks were filled with gunpowder in times of war so that they could be blown up along with any enemy troops that managed to penetrate the fortifications. This happened in 1626 to 300 Spanish soldiers from the army of the von Hessen-Darmstadt family. A look around the well-equipped **Burgmuseum** also gives a good idea of the former size of the whole construction. A model of the fortress in the former chapel shows clearly how strong its defensive position was, especially on the north side which was the main side of attack. It was possible to reconstruct the buildings exactly because in around 1607 a land surveyor called Schäfer, known as Dilich, was commissioned by Landgrave Moritz to make detailed drawings in colour along with sectional views and lay-out plans of the whole structure.

Open to the public April - October, with or without guided tours. Tours last 1¼ hours. Car park next to the castle. Climb up from St. Goar 10 min.

Original Tower of Rheinfels ruins and High Battery.

Rheinfels: View of the castle with its high Darmstädter Bau.

Burg Maus above Wellmich

Within view of Burg Katz and situated above St. Goarshausen-Wellmich stands Burg **«Maus»**. It was given this nickname because its neighbour Katz (cat) Castle was owned by the powerful Katzenelnbogen family, who only seemed to be waiting for a favourable opportunity to pounce on the «Maus» (mouse). The castle, which was completed in 1356 under the Archbishop of Trier Kuno von Falkenstein, was considered one of the most advanced and best fortified in its time. The Thurnburg or Theuerburg, to use its proper name, for a time was the residence of the

Burg «Maus» above Wellmich. The Electoral Trier castle «Thurnberg» (1356) was given this name because of its proximity to Burg «Katz».

archbishops of Trier. Napoleon had it blown up in 1806 as part of his campaign to destroy all of the Rhine fortifications. Fortunately the magnificent structure was rebuilt in 1900-1906 in accordance with the original plans.
The almost square outer wall widens on the side towards the hill, where the moat is, into a curtain wall, surpassed by the mighty

round keep near the outer wall. Opposite it is a four-storey tower with living quarters. Here, as well as in the imposing Palas (Hall) next to it, corner-bays emphasize the excellent fortifications of the whole structure. Together with the dainty round-arch frieze, they are at the same time attractive decorative elements within a harmoniously designed construction. The valuable interior with its extensive collections from the time of the reconstruction of the castle make it really worth a visit. The splendid view of the Rhine valley also makes up for the steep climb.

Open all year round. Road up from Wellmich. Footpath 25 min.

The small town of **Wellmich** is today part of St. Goarshausen. It already had the statuts of a town when the castle was completed in 1356. At about the same time the Gothic parish church was built, one of the most beautiful in the Middle Rhine area, with a wonderful chancel. One of the most interesting Late Gothic statues in the church is a Pietà (around 1450). A magnificent fresco showing the Day of Judgement also dates back to the 15th century. On the outer wall of the vestry there is a painted sandstone masterpiece of the Crucifixion.

Downstream, opposite Hirzenach, we see the parish of **Kestert**. From here there are footpaths up to the look-out point called Hindenburghöhe. Further down the Rhine we pass through the small town of Bad Salzig, a well-known spa with thermal springs and a modern spa clinic.

View of Bad Salzig, a spa with hot springs. At the front the Wallfahrtskirche (13th century) in Bornhofen.

Kamp-Bornhofen and the «Hostile Brothers»

Passing the castles of Sterrenberg and Liebenstein, known as «the hostile brothers», we arrive at Kamp-Bornhofen. On the way up to the castles, we pass **Kloster Bornhofen** (1679-84). The old 13th century pilgrims' church was given its present appearance at the beginning of the 15th century. A Passion picture shows members of Rhenish aristocratic families as sponsors and donors. At the beginning of the 20th century, when the

Kamp-Bornhofen and the «hostile brothers» Sterrenberg and Liebenstein. Below the Wallfahrtskirche and Kloster Bornhofen.

church was no longer able to accommodate all the pilgrims, the Franciscan monks had a beautiful pilgrims' place laid out on the north side in 1912, and then, in 1932/33 an even larger one with room for 5,000 pilgrims.

The one time rich contents of the monastery were given by the Herzog (Duke) von Nassau in 1813 to the parish of St. Boniface in Wiesbaden. The only thing left was the Miraculous Image. The partly whitewashed Burg **Sterrenberg** came into existence in the

54

11th century as a Reichsburg. In 1248 the Burggraf von Sterrenberg had the wooden house 30 m above the fortress extended into an outwork which later bacame Burg **Liebenstein**.

At the same time the burgrave had the 2.5 m thick outer curtain wall between the castle and the outwork put up. Although this was originally intended to improve the defences of both castles, at first sight it seems to be directed menacingly against Liebenstein Castle. This gave the wall its nickname «wall of conflict». The second castle also has a moat and fortified walls with embrasures on the side facing Sterrenberg Castle. No wonder people gave the castles the nickname «the hostile brothers». Sterrenberg Castle was protected on three sides by its location on top of a rocky crag; the fourth side was for-

Miraculous Image in the Wallfahrtskirche in Bornhofen, the destination of many pilgrims since the 13th century

tified with two curtain walls, a moat and gates. Nevertheless the buildings were described as being in decay as early as 1568 and used as a quarry. Recent modifications have made it possible for the two castles to be used as restaurants. The «Sterrenberg» received its original colour a few years ago – white with red brickwork.

Burg Sterrenberg, built as an Imperial Castle in the 11th century. The outer curtain wall looking towards the former outwork Liebenstein has the nickname «wall of conflict».

55

Kamp-Bornhofen. «Der von der Leyensche Hof», a typical Rhenish Renaissance building.

After the line of the «Schenken von Liebenstein» had died out, the earlier castle went in 1783 as Nassau fief to Baron «von Preuschen» whose successors still own it.

Both castles open to the public daily. Car parks near the castles. Footpath from Bornhofen 30 min.

The district of **Kamp** was first mentioned in 1138, and until about 1315 it was subject to the Emperor alone. Then the town and the castles passed into the possession of Electoral Trier until 1802. The town centre has many historic half-timbered houses, especially in the Rheinuferstrasse and Kreuzstrasse. Of the mediaeval St. Nicholas parish church (1251) only the tower remains standing; the rest had to make way for a new building in Neo-Gothic style in 1902. The pulpit, however, was part of the original church. Opposite the main door of St. Nicholas' Church we see the beautiful portal of the Augustinian convent with a statue of St. Augustine. The date shown (1732) is the year in which the original convent was renovated as it stands today. The convent itself was dissolved in 1802. In the Schmiedgasse we find the «Von der Leyensche Hof», a typical example of Rhenish Renaissance.

Boppard

Diagonally across from Kamp-Bornhofen, just before the narrow horse-shoe bend in the Rhine lies the old Imperial town of Boppard. In the 4th century the Romans replaced their citadel by a stone fortress with 28 towers, which, however, was soon overrun by Germanic tribes. Today no other German town has such well-preserved Roman fortress ruins as Boppard. The former Free Imperial City was subjugated in 1327 by the elector Balduin von Trier, after King Heinrich VII had pawned it away to his brother, the Elector, 15 years earlier. Balduin immediately had the Electoral Trier castle built, thereby forcing the uncooperative inhabitants to accept his rule. A walk around this extremely interesting town could well at the **Carmelite Church** (started in 1319) in the Rheinallee. It contains two 17th century altars, numerous tombstones of local noble families, and a statue of the Virgin Mary (1330) called the «Traubenmadonna». The 5th century tombstone of a child's grave, the so-called «Armeniusstein», is one of the oldest Christian monuments. The Baroque building further up was completed in 1730 as a monastery and is now used by the

Boppard, an old Imperial Town, with well-preserved remains of a Roman city wall (4th century). The chair-lift goes up to the lookout-point «Vierseenblick».

town council. The cloisters surround a spacious courtyard with an attractive Germanic pillar fountain. The Karmeliterstrasse and the Oberstrasse take us on to the Kirchgasse. The Gothic archway to the left once belonged to the «Danzhus» (15th century). At the Angertstrasse junction we discover on the right-hand side parts of the Roman wall with the remains of a tower. We follow the road on the left to the Binger Tor, part of the mediaeval town fortifications. Up on a hill we see the Baroque building of the former Marienburg Convent (1740). The Casinostrasse leads us down the Rheinallee, which takes us back into town. A strong wall, called the «Eisbrech» (Icebreaker) used to con-

Boppard by night. The St. Severus Church (1150-1326). The floor of the church contains the outline of the baptismal font and the pulpit of the original 5th century church.

nect the Sandtor with the river. The Gothic town hall next to it was once inhabited by the Ritter von Schwalbach, whose tomb-stones we noticed in the Carmelite Church. We walk past the former Franciscan monastery (17th century) and a stately Baroque house with a coat-of-arms on the balcony railing. All that is left of the original Electoral Trier castle is the keep. The tombstones and the statue in the inner courtyard are from St. Severus Church. The castle today houses a folk museum. Behind the castle is the

The «Vierseenblick» (view of four lakes) from the lookout point above Boppard. On the left beside the hill on the bend lies Osterspai.

Burggasse we discover 15 m of the old **Roman wall** by the **Römerburg»** Hotel. Continuing along the Untere Marktstrasse we arrive at **St. Severus Church,** which contains a painted ceiling from around 1200 as well as an artistically valuable triumphal cross above the altar (13th century). The Kronengasse and Kronentor then take us past picturesque half-timbered houses and back to the Rheinallee.

A cable railway goes up to one of the most famous look-out points along the Rhine, the **«Vierseenblick»,** overlooking four lakes at once. On our way up and down we have a wonderful view of the biggest horse-shoe bend along the Rhine.

The big horse-shoe bend near Boppard. The railway and the road follow the river round the hill on the bend.

Braubach and the Marksburg

Leaving Boppard, the river, the roads and the railway wind round a narrow horse-shoe bend. At the end of the steep right-hand bend lies the village of Osterspai with its small, fortified 13th century castle. The tower containing living quarters, which was added in the 14th century, is still standing today. The Ba-

Braubach and Marksburg fortress (12th century). The dark, solid tower in the middle of town was once part of the town's mediaeval fortifications; since the 14th century it has been part of the Early Gothic St. Barbara's Church.

roque castle above the village is called Liebeneck (17th century). At Spay, on the left-hand side, after a left bend, the Rhine regains its northwesterly direction. On a wooded peak on the right-hand side stands the imposing Marksburg above the town of **Braubach**. Burial grounds indicate that this area has been inhabited since about 500 BC. It was first mentioned in the 7th century. The Herren von Eppstein, who had been given a Palatinate fief, built the castle and were the owners of the town in the 12th century. Their successors in 1283 were the powerful Grafen von Katzenelnbogen, who also took over the levying of customs duties in Braubach (until 1325). When they died out in 1479, their possessions went to the Landgrafen von Hessen (until 1803). The **Phi-**

Braubach: Obertor and remains of the town wall.

lippsburg at the southern entrance to the town was built by Philipp II von Hessen-Rheinfels in 1568-71 as a secondary residence. When he died, his widow used it as a place of retreat. Its «golden age» was after 1643, when Johann der Streitbare kept court here in a magnificent style. Passing through the castle gates we find ourselves in the romantic castle yard of this attractive castle.

Down beside the Rhine the visitor should not miss seeing the famous rose gardens. The tower of the Early Gothic St. Barbara's Church (14th century) was erected around 1200 and was part of the town's defences. Built-in fire-places and benches suggest that it probably used to be inhabited. The town fortifications included the Marksburg. In the town itself, the Obertor, the Pankgrafenturm and parts of the town wall are still standing. The centre of the town is full of old-world charm in which we come across picturesque corners and narrow streets with their attractive half-timbered houses.

When Napoleon reorganized the map of Germany, Braubach, which until then had been part of Hessen, went to the Duchy of Nassau in 1803, and then to Prussia in 1866. In 1900 Prussia sold the **Marksburg** for a symbolic 1000 Reichsmarks to the German Castles Association, which it still belongs today. Its excellent location on a high wooded peak made any kind of attack seemed doomed to failure. Perhaps as a result of

View of Marksburg fortress, the only Knight's castle along the Rhine still standing

this, it was never attacked or besieged in spite of its strategic position on the Rhine, and is therefore the only castle on the Rhine that dates back to Knighthood days. Barred windows bear witness to the fact that for a long time under the administration of Hessen and Nassau it was a state prison.

Walking up from Braubach or just from the large car park below the castle, we come to the first of the five gates, the drawbridge gate. In the 17th century it was reinforced by a tunnel passage, 25 m long, with mighty barrel vaults and a sharp bend in it for defence purposes. Seven guns also contributed to its defensive strenght. The outer bailey leads us on to the Fuchstor (14th century), which has a sally-gate for counter-attack purposes. Beneath the wooden bridge, which could be removed in times of danger, there was a pitfall. Crossing the inner bailey, we arrive at the embrasure gate with the castellan's tower. A staircase hewn into the rock leads beneath the Big Battery – on the Zollbachtal side – to the battery yard. An iron gate finally admits us to the triangular inner yard of the castle. In the centre of this stands the 39 m high keep. Its square 6 x 6 m base was part of the original castle built around 1200, the narrow tower was added in the 14th century. Originally it was only possible to enter it eight metres up via ladder. Prisoners were thrown into the dungeon six metres below through the «Angstloch» (Hole of Fear). Additional floors were added to the Romanesque Palas (Hall) on the north side after a fire in 1705. In the cellar, which used to be the stables, the present owner, the Castles Association, gives us an idea of mediaeval justice in the «torture chamber» containing a collection of torture and punishment instruments. To the right is the 27 m long Gothic hall with its impressive kitchen and open fire-place. Deep window recesses show how thick the curtain wall is (3 m). On the upper floor were the ladies' rooms and the 65 m² knights' hall with latrine bays in the outer wall. On the side overlooking the Rhine there is a half-timbered building put up in 1705 to replace the bakery, the well and the water-tank. This building today contains a weaving-room and an armoury – with an exhibition

Marksburg: Armoury. Display of mediaeval armour and weapons.

on «Armament over the Ages». The first floor of the Chapel Tower (built around 1200) is taken up by the Markuskapelle (Saint Mark's Chapel), which gave the former «Burg Braubach» its present name. In the upper bailey the present owners have planted a herb garden containing all the seasoning and medicinal herbs used in the Middle Ages among other things for witches' brews and magic potions. The castle also houses a unique library with 12,000 volumes on castles and castle history.

Marksburg: Castle kitchen in the Gothic Hall building. A whole ox on a spit could be roasted over the huge open fireplace.

The outworks «Pulvereck» and «Scharfes Eck» were added in the 17th century to reinforce the castle's defences. After 1900 the Castles Association had the whole neglected structure restored according to engravings made by the surveyor Dilich. Above the drawbridge gate – aside from the main buildings – they added a castle restaurant.
Open daily. Footpath from Braubach 25 min., from the car park 5 min.

The Königsstuhl near Rhens

Downstream from Braubach on the left bank of the Rhine lies the little town of Rhens, once situated at the meeting point of four Rhenish electors' territories. It was in an orchard here that the archbishops of Cologne, Mainz and Trier and the Elector of the Palatinate chose Rudolf von Habsburg as Emperor in 1273. The town became famous by the «Kurverein von Rhense», which agreed in 1338 that a king chosen by electors no longer needed confirmation by the Pope. It was here in Rhens that Karl IV was elected king in 1346 and Ruprecht von der Pfalz – the last one – in 1400. On the bank of the Rhine 300 m downstream, a building was erected at the end of the 14th century – the Königsstuhl.
Ruprecht's successors, elected in Frankfurt, showed themselves to the people and took their oath of allegiance here before being crowned in Aachen. The building was pulled down at the beginning of the last century but rebuilt 50 years later. The new building, now located on a hill beside the road from Rhens to Waldesch, is based on the original mediaeval one and can be considered a historic German monument.

Schloss Stolzenfels

Opposite where the River Lahn joins the Rhine and upstream from the town of Kapellen on a rocky peak stands Schloss Stolzenfels. It was built by the Archbishop of Trier Arnold von Isenburg (1242-59) only a few years after the Elector of Mainz had had Burg Lahneck put up opposite. Both castles were given the right to collect customs duties on the Rhine in the 14th century. During the unsuccessful siege of Koblenz in 1688/89 Stolzenfels was burnt to the ground by the French and left as a ruin and a quarry. The town of Koblenz gave it to Crown Prince Friedrich Wilhelm von Preussen in 1823, who had it rebuilt and extended after designs by the famous architect Schinkel. The mediaeval structure with its keep, its building overlooking the Rhine, its walls and outer bailey, remained more or less as before, but, by adding the buildings on the other side towards the hill, Schinkel created a symmetrical lay-out. The flat roofs have battlements around them like English castles. The whole construction is considered a perfect example of Rhenish Late Romanticism.
The living quarters of the King of Prussia and his wife covered both wings of the first floor. We can still admire the valuable furniture in those seven rooms, including precious antiques such as the finely crafted desk once belonging to the Elector of Trier (around 1700). A wide staircase leads us from the castle

yard through the arcades to the Mediterranean-style pergola garden with its fountain and Adjutantenturm (Adjutant's Tower) (14th century) at the far end. A gateway takes us on to the great Rhine terrace. The fountain proudly displays a Prussian eagle. The outer wall painting shows the reception of Ruprecht von der Pfalz chosen king in Rhens in 1400. Standing aside from the castle itself, the Klausengebäude (1843) with its servants' quarters, stables and coach-houses was obviously influenced in style by English Late Gothic.

Footpath 15 min. from Kapellen, a romantic serpentine pathway with a viaduct. Open 1.1. to 30.11. except Monday.

Schloss Stolzenfels: On the foundations of a knight's castle (13th century), the Crown Prince of Prussia had an English-looking castle built in Rhenish Late Romaticist style.

Burg Lahneck and Lahnstein

The area around the mouth of the River Lahn was already settled on in 4000 BC. The Electoral Mainz' **Burg Lahneck** was built in around 1240 to defend the nearby silver mines and as the northernmost bastion in the country. In the 15th century, the castle's fortifications were improved to make it able to deal with the new firearms – on each side of the old keep, a 3.5 m thick curtain wall was added. In 1688 the castle was laid in ruins by the French, then from 1852 onwards rebuilt in New Gothic style incorporating all that was left standing of the original castle. The castle con-

Burg Lahneck above Lahnstein. The keep is flanked by 3.5 m thick curtain walls on the side of attack. Opposite lies Schloss Stolzenfels, and, on the mouth of the Lahn, Niederlahnstein.

tains a delightful chapel, a Rittersaal (Knight's Hall) particularly worth seeing, as well as valuable pictures and furnitures. From the keep we are able to enjoy a magnificent panorama.

In addition to this, **Oberlahnstein** also has a second castle right beside the Rhine, built in the 14th century by Electoral Mainz as a customs fortress. The oldest part of the **Martinsburg** is its hexagonal keep. Some parts of the town fortifications are still standing, the Hexenturm (Witches' Tower) now contains a historic assembly room and a museum. In around 1160 the Romanesque Salhof was built, which is now a tourist office. In the Hochstrasse we still find a number of historic residences, but also the old Town Hall (around 1507), a Gothic half-timbered building.

Niederlahnstein: the famous «Wirtshaus an der Lahn» (1697)

Niederlahnstein, part of the town of Lahnstein since 1969, has the oldest gallery church in the middle Rhine area, the Romanesque Johanniskirche (St. John's Church), which was built from 950 onwards and redesigned with alternations added in 1130. In the Johannisstrasse we find the Märkerhof (13th century) and the Gasthaus «Schwanen» (1664). Not quite as old but all the more famous, the **«Wirtshaus an der Lahn»** (an inn beside the River Lahn) (1697) was already mentioned in Goethe's writings.

Tucked away in the park at the eastern end of the district stands the Arnsteiner Hof (16th century), which contains a dainty little Gothic chapel. A modern spa centre has been built above the urban part of Lahnstein.

Burg Lahneck open to the public April - October. Restaurant open all year round. Open-air theatre performances August/September. Castle car park. 20 minutes to walk from the bus-stop.

Oberlahnstein: Martinsburg. The Electors of Mainz had the customs fortress erected beside the Rhine in about 1300.

Koblenz and Ehrenbreitstein fortress

After the fall of the frontier fortification «Limes», the fortified Roman town of «Confluentes» became of great strategic importance as a frontier fortress. Pile bridges over the Moselle and the Rhine provided links with neighbouring regions. The Franconians replaced the ruined Roman settlement by a Royal Court (5th century). In 1018 Koblenz and the castle Ehrenbreitstein were given to the archbishops of Trier. It was here that Konrad III von Hohenstaufen was elected Emperor in 1138, and that a meeting of princes was held in 1338. In spite of the fact that Koblenz lost two-thirds of its buildings in an unsuccessful siege by Ludwig XIV's armies, the archbishops made it their residence. Under Prussian rule (from 1815 onwards) the town was turned onto a fortress, the Electoral Palace became a subsidiary residence. Today Koblenz, a city since 1962, is the home of a large garrison and has made a name for itself as a wine-growing town.

The promenades along the Rhine and the Moselle, altogether 8 km long, meet at the **«Deutsches Eck»,** a good starting-point for a walk round the **Old City.** This point where the Moselle flows into the Rhine was given its name after 1216 when the Deutschordensritter established a settlement nearby. In a charming gar-

Koblenz: Ehrenbreitstein fortress, built since 1817, as a substitute for the Electoral Trier fortress destroyed in 1799.

Koblenz: The «Plan». In the background the Baroque towers of the Liebfrauen-kirche (started in the 12th century), the most striking landmark in the town's silhouette.

den park stands at the well-preserved Komptur-haus (Commander's House). The Kastor Church, consecrated in 836, is one of the most impressive Romanesque churches, and contains many works of art. In the Kastorstrasse we notice a tower with battlements, the so-called «Deutscher Kaiser». What is today the vicarage of «Our Lady» was built on the site of the Royal Court (5th century). The towers behind it are remains of the Roman town fortifications (4th century). Another Roman tower can be seen in the walls of the Gothic chancel of the Florinskirche (12th century). The buildings that stand out most along the romantic banks of the Moselle are the old castle (from the 13th century onwards), today the town library, and the stone Balduin's Bridge with its fourteen arches, built under Elector Balduin (1307-54). In the Liebfrauenkirche (Church of Our Lady) in the centre of the old town we find an unexpectedly harmonious combination of Romanesque, Gothic and Baroque architecture. Looking around, we see attractive façades, e.g. at the «Altes Kaufhaus», the «Plan», and in the Löhrstrasse. One of the town's landmarks is in the courtyard of the town hall, which used to be a Jesuit College: the Schöngelbrunnen (1940) with a bronze fountain depicting a boy from Koblenz. The spacious palace near the Rhine promenade was built by Elector Clemens Wenzelslaus in 1786 in Classicist style. Near the Rhine bridge, the town had a further tourist attraction built in

Koblenz: Deutsches Eck. The spit of land where the Moselle and Rhine meet got its name from the Deutschordensritter (Knights) who settled nearby in 1216.

1925, the Weindorf (Wine Village). This is an exact reproduction of a wine-growing village, giving visitors from all over the world an opportunity to enjoy the produce of German winegrowers in a romantic and typically Rhine-Moselle atmosphere.

From its 118 m high terrace opposite the mouth of the Moselle, **Ehrenbreitstein** castle and fortress has a commanding position over such a strategically important part of the Rhine valley. The first castle was built by a certain «Ehrenbert» at the end of the 10th century, a nobleman probably from the Salian-Carolingian house. From the 16th century onwards the Trier rulers had it made into a fortress, which was regarded as being invicible until about 1800. In 1688 and 1794-99, it withstood five sieges by French troops. At the end of 1799, however, they managed to take the fortress by starving out the occupants, after which they demolished it with 30,000 pounds of gunpowder. The present fortress was erected from 1817 on by the Prussians in Classicist style. Rounded archways with carefully finished openings, capitals, blind arcades and accentuated horizontal joints contrast with the simple, monumental façade of this functional building. Once a year the fortress and the town of Koblenz are illuminated with Bengal lights as part of the great firework display **«Rhein in Flammen»** (The Rhine on Fire).

Car parks near the fortress _ Chair-lift.

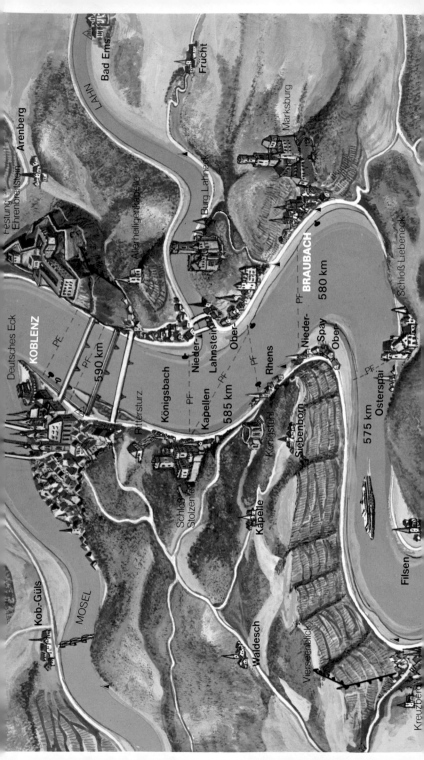

Festung
Ehrenbreitstein

Arenberg

Bad Ems

LAHN

Frücht

Deutsches Eck

Marksburg

Allerheiligenkapelle

Burg Lahneck

KOBLENZ

PF

590 km

PF

PF

Nieder-

Lahnstein

Ober-

BRAUBACH

580 km

Rittersturz

Königsbach

Schloß Liebeneck

Nieder-

PF

Kapellen

PF

Rhens

Nieder-

Spay

Ober-

585 km

PF

Schloß
Stolzenfels

Königstuhl

Siebenborn

PF

Osterspai

Kob.-Güls

MOSEL

Kapelle

575 km

Waldesch

Vierseenblick

Filsen

Kreuzberg

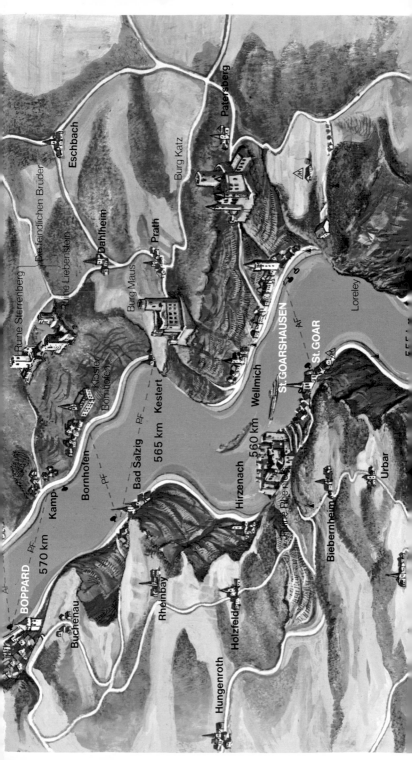

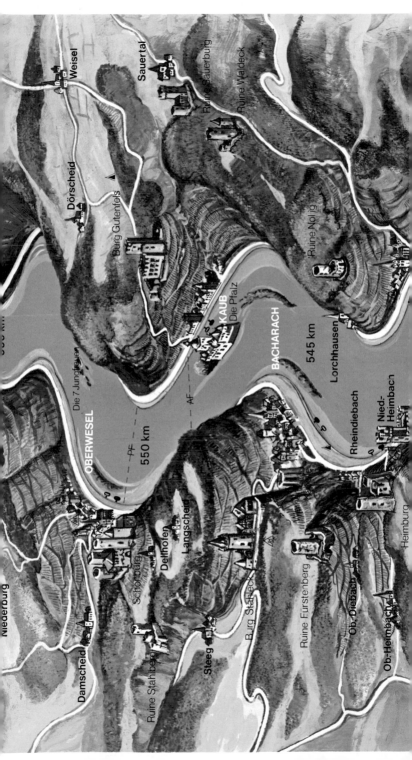

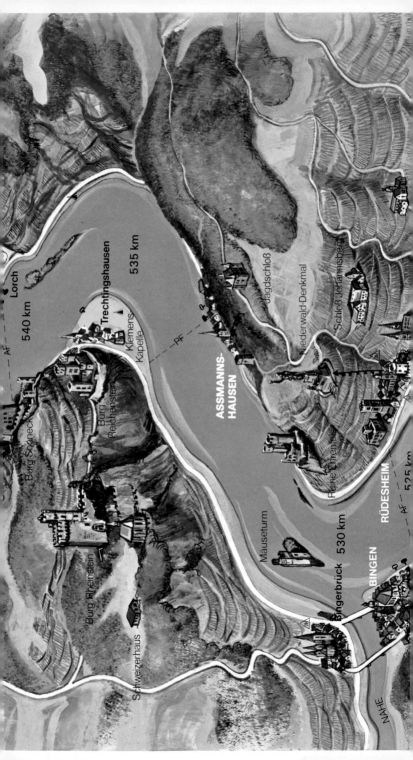

MAIN

500 km

MAINZ

Biebrich

WIESBADEN

Kloster-Eberbach

ELTVILLE

510 km

505 km

Östrich

515 km

Winkel

Mittelheim

Geisenheim

520 km

Budenheim

Frei-Weinheim

Ingelheim

Heidesheim

Gonsenheim

Bretzenheim

Rochus-Kapelle

Burg Klopp

Wackernheim

Marienborn

Drais

Gau-Algesheim

Ockenheim

Key:

- Landing stages of the ‹Köln-Düsseldorfer›
  Schiffahrtsgesellschaft
- Other landing stages
- Passenger-ferry
- Car ferry
- Youth hostels
- Camping sites